The Egg- and Dairy-Free
Cookbook

Skyhorse Publishing books may be purchased in bulk at special
discounts for sales promotion, corporate gifts, fund-raising, or
educational purposes. Special editions can also be created to
specifications. For details, contact the Special Sales Department,
Skyhorse Publishing, 307 West 36th Street, 11th Floor,
New York, NY 10018 or info@skyhorsepublishing.com.

Skyhorse® and Skyhorse Publishing® are registered trademarks of
Skyhorse Publishing, Inc.®, a Delaware corporation.

www.skyhorsepublishing.com

10 9 8 7 6 5 4 3 2 1

Library of Congress Cataloging-in-Publication Data is available on file.

ISBN: 978-1-62087-213-0

Printed in the United States of America

The Egg- and Dairy-Free Cookbook

50 Delicious Recipes for the Whole Family

ANNA BENCKERT & PERNILLA WARNHAMMAR

Translation by Stine Skarpnes Osttveit

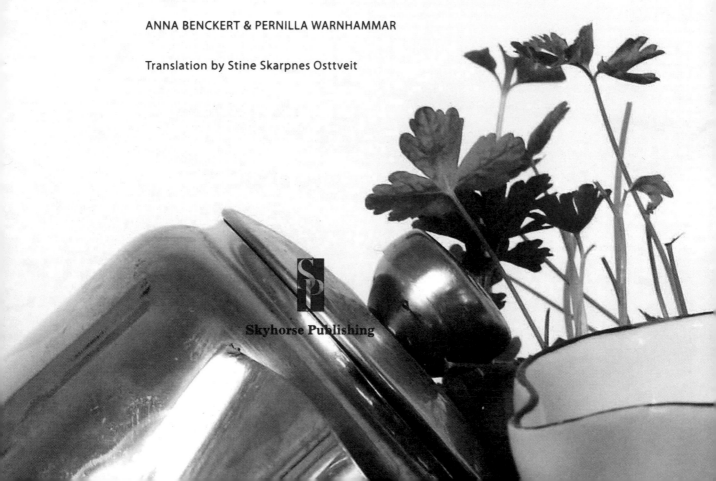

Skyhorse Publishing

Table of Contents

A cookbook for everyone

We, the authors, have children with lactose intolerance, and we've struggled with it ourselves. We want to share our experiences and share with you our simple and varied recipes, which we've gathered over the years. There's no reason why you shouldn't eat and enjoy great food because you have an allergy.

Reality

Daily, we are confronted with having to think of simple, nutritious, and tasty dinners that can satisfy each family member. We skim through tiny ingredient lists in the hopes that the product won't contain milk or eggs; and still we come home from the grocery store with very few products that everyone can eat. And we ask ourselves why there are so many additives in all of these foods today.

To live in a family with food allergies

To stand at the grocery store with tired children tugging at your clothes while trying to think of what to buy for dinner is a challenge. Parents of children without food allergies often have the same feeling, but on the other hand, they have a much larger selection of processed products to choose from. But there are downsides to processed foods. Most often they do not taste as good as homemade food, and they're not always as nutritious as a meal made from carefully selected raw materials.

One or two meals?

Maybe you are allergic or you have a family member with an allergy. As mentioned, it is usually the children in our families that have allergies. This means that we either have to make two meals each night, or we have to make one meal with the same ingredients for everyone. The latter seems easier. Not to mention the fact that it's more enjoyable when the children eat the same food as the rest of the family. In our opinion, there are too many other occasions where the children have to eat differently than the rest of us, for instance parties or at cafés.

The best tip—plan ahead!

Financially and time-wise, it makes sense to plan dinners and shopping lists one week in advance. It is not as hard to change one's eating habits as one might think. It is all about finding a routine. The children adapt quite quickly and see that you prioritize eating together, which again leads to a tasty and cozy dinner. It's a moment during the day when the whole family can get together and spend time with each other.

Balance

It turns out that when we plan and prepare meals we also have more energy and time to spare. As parents, we are more alert since it's not as tiresome to make the dinners when they're already planned out, and the children eat willingly because they enjoy sitting down at the dinner table. We also have a better financial overview of our food expenses as opposed to making several trips to the grocery store every week.

Good to keep at home

If you keep a certain number of basic ingredients at home, you should be able to whip up a meal out of almost anything. These basic ingredients will, of course, vary from family to family; however, those listed here work well for our families.

In the cupboard

For flavor
As many spices as possible
Bouillon cubes

Dry ingredients
Baking powder
Natural egg replacer
Various kinds of flour
Breadcrumbs
Pasta
Bulgur
Couscous
Quinoa
Rice

Liquids
Olive oil
White wine vinegar
Balsamic vinegar
Honey

Preserved foods
Black and green olives
Crushed tomatoes
Anchovies
Chickpeas

Additionally...
Oat milk and/or soy milk

On the kitchen counter

Fresh foods
As many herb varieties as possible
Lots of fresh fruit

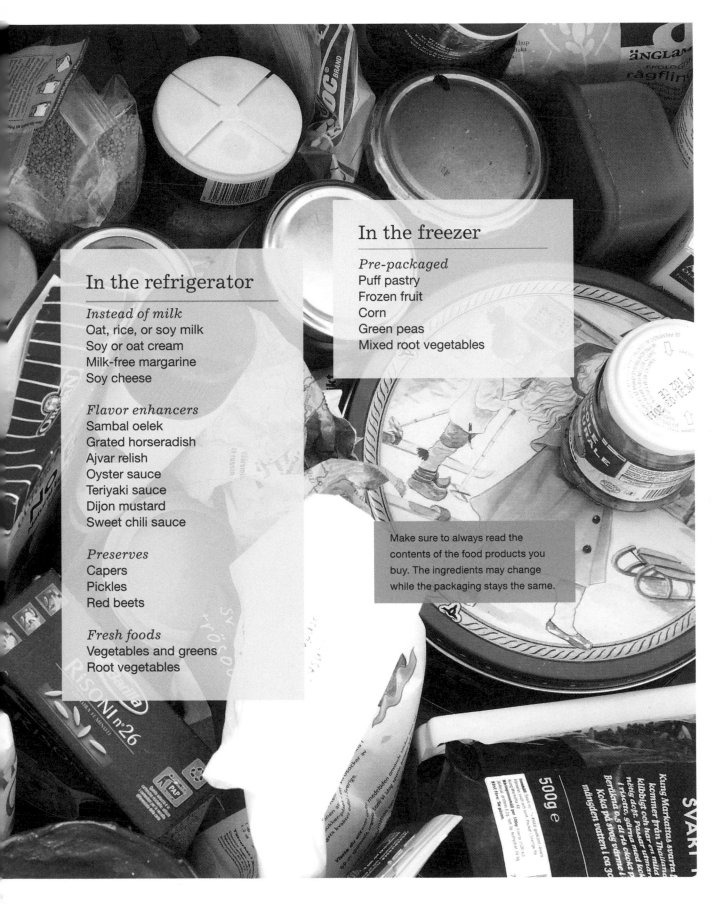

In the refrigerator

Instead of milk
Oat, rice, or soy milk
Soy or oat cream
Milk-free margarine
Soy cheese

Flavor enhancers
Sambal oelek
Grated horseradish
Ajvar relish
Oyster sauce
Teriyaki sauce
Dijon mustard
Sweet chili sauce

Preserves
Capers
Pickles
Red beets

Fresh foods
Vegetables and greens
Root vegetables

In the freezer

Pre-packaged
Puff pastry
Frozen fruit
Corn
Green peas
Mixed root vegetables

Make sure to always read the
contents of the food products you
buy. The ingredients may change
while the packaging stays the same.

Fish and shellfish

Fried herring
stuffed with olives and sage

4 Servings

Either you love this, or you just can't understand how some people are so enthused by a couple of herring filets. To us, there is nothing better than fried herring, homemade mashed potatoes, and lingonberries.

Take the butter out of the refrigerator and let it sit in room temperature. Peel the potatoes and place them on the stove for boiling. Rinse the fish filets and set them aside.

Roughly chop the olives and sage and mix them in with the margarine. Spread a tablespoon of the mixture on half of the fish filets. Top with the rest of the filets. Prepare the mashed potatoes so that they are ready to serve once the fish is fried. Mash the boiled potatoes with a mixer or by hand. Warm the oat or soy milk. Add the margarine and the warm milk to the potatoes. Flavor with salt and pepper and mix well.

Blend breadcrumbs, flour, salt, and pepper and place the mix on a plate large enough to turn the fresh filets in. Coat the herring filets with the mixture. Fry the fish in butter on low heat, a couple of minutes on each side. Pour the rest of the butter gravy on top of the fried filets. Serve with mashed potatoes and lingonberries.

5 tbsp milk-free margarine
about 16 herring filets
1 can lemon olives
1 pot fresh sage
4 tbsp milk-free breadcrumbs
2 tbsp flour
salt
pepper

10 large potatoes
5 tbsp milk-free margarine
about 1 cup (250 ml) oat or soy milk
salt
pepper

lingonberries, or cranberries

Rich French fish soup

14 oz fish pieces
(cod, salmon, pollock)
2 carrots
2 potatoes
1 yellow onion
½ leek
1 celery root
1 parsnip
1 box of plum tomatoes (14 oz/400 g)
1 tbsp fish sauce (optional)
2 tsp curry
salt and pepper
1 handful of fresh thyme
2 cubes of fish bouillon
3 cups (750 ml) water
½ cup (70 g) soy or oat cream (optional)

Sauce
1 cup (110 g) soy yogurt
2 tbsp egg-free mayonnaise
2 tbsp tomato paste
1 tsp sambal oelek
1 garlic clove

4 servings

Frozen fish is great in this soup. You will usually be able to find cubed frozen fish in grocery stores. If you leave the fish in the refrigerator in the morning it will be ready to use by evening.

Slice the peeled carrots into ¼-inch (½-cm) thick pieces. Peel and slice potatoes, onion, celery root, and parsnip into equally sized pieces. Blend soy yogurt, mayonnaise, tomato paste, and sambal oelek. Add 1 pressed garlic clove.

Brown the vegetables in a large pot with a thick bottom. They do not have to be fried all the way through. They will finish cooking later on while the soup is simmering. Add tomatoes and spices.

Blend the bouillon cubes to 1 cup (250 ml) of boiled water and add it to the root vegetable mix. Add the remaining amount of water and let the soup simmer for about 20 minutes.

Make sure the vegetables are ready. Add, if you wish, oat or soy cream for a thicker consistency. Lastly, add the thawed fish. Let the soup stew for about 5 minutes until the fish is cooked all the way through. Serve with the sauce and tasty bread for dipping.

Risoni, lime, shrimp, and chili

4 servings

Risoni is pasta shaped like rice, and this is a spicy pasta salad.

Fresh shrimps are peeled and set aside. If you bought shrimps in a jar, drain them in a sieve for at least 10 minutes.

Bring water to a boil for the risoni. You boil the risoni the same way you would any other kind of pasta. Rinse and chop the bell pepper, tomatoes, leek, and apple while the pasta is boiling. Stir these together to make a dressing. Carefully remove the cores of the chili before you slice it thinly. Squeeze the lime with a fork.

When the risoni is ready, drain it in a sieve. Drizzle some olive oil on top so that the pasta isn't sticky.

Toss together all of the ingredients and serve with the dressing.

½ lb (250 g) shrimp
1 pack of risoni
1 bell pepper
2 tomatoes
½ leek
1 red apple
2 tbsp olive oil or sunflower oil
salt
pepper
fresh herbs

Dressing
1 cup (110 g) soy yogurt
2 tbsp lime juice
1 fresh chili
salt
pepper

Oven-baked salmon on a bed of salt

4 servings

1 half of fresh salmon 5–7 oz
(150–200 g) per person
1 packet of coarse salt
potatoes

Sauce
1½ cups (300 g) soy crème fraiche
2 tbsp egg-free mayonnaise
1 can of salmon roe
1 lemon
salt
pepper

An incredibly simple dish that really only needs quality raw ingredients to turn out great. This is perfect for dinner parties with many guests. Try to get a hold of half of a fresh salmon. If you have leftovers it will taste great the next day as well.

Set the oven to 210°F (100°C). Rinse the fish and dry it off with a paper towel. Cover the bottom of a baking pan with salt. Place the salmon on top of the salt bed with the skin facing downwards. Bake in the oven for 1 hour. Boil the potatoes and prepare the cold crème fraiche sauce while the fish is baking.

Stir soy crème fraiche, mayonnaise, and salmon roe together in a bowl. Flavor the sauce with lemon juice, salt, and pepper.

Mussels boiled in beer with homemade French fries

1 batch of blue mussels
2 yellow onions
olive or canola oil
1 bottle of dark beer
salt

firm potatoes
olive or sunflower oil
salt

Mayonnaise sauce
1 cup (210 g) soy crème fraiche
2 tbsp egg-free mayonnaise
salt
pepper
a few drops of lemon

4 servings

Rinse and scrape the mussels. Throw out any that are broken or that don't close if you carefully tap them against the kitchen counter.

Set the oven to 435°F (225°C). Peel and cut the potatoes in narrow strips. Place the sliced potatoes in a plastic bag with oil and salt, and shake. This way the olive oil is evenly distributed, and you prevent the slices from sticking together. Place the potato slices in a baking pan and bake in the oven for about 20 minutes.

Blend soy crème fraiche and mayonnaise to make a sauce. Salt, pepper, and flavor the sauce with a few drops of lemon.

Chop the onions and brown in the oil until soft, but not burnt. Right before the French fries are done, place the mussels in the onions and pour the beer over them. Boil for 5 minutes or until the mussels open. Serve right away.

Blinis
with fisherman's gold

4 servings

Crumble the yeast in a large bowl. Warm the soy or oat milk to 98°F (37°C). Stir a couple of tablespoons of the milk in with the yeast so that the yeast dissolves. Add in the rest of the milk alternative and the remaining ingredients and let it rise in room temperature for 1 hour.

Fry the blinis in milk-free margarine on medium heat in a cast-iron pancake pan. Peel and chop the onion while they fry.

Serve the blinis warm with a spoonful of roe, finely-chopped onion, and tofu crème fraiche or soy yogurt.

1⅓ tbsp (25 g) yeast
2½ cups (625 ml) soy or oat milk
1 cup (120 g) buckwheat flour
1 cup (120 g) wheat flour
½ tsp salt
milk-free margarine (for frying)

Topping
3 shallots or 1 red onion
1 can roe
4 tbsp tofu crème fraiche
or soy yogurt

Italian fish cakes with lemon and capers

1 cup (250 ml) water

4 tbsp milk-free crumbled bread

4 anchovies

½ cup (60 g) pickles

1⅓ lbs (600 g) fish

2 tbsp capers

salt

pepper

2 tbsp olive oil (for frying)

salad

lemon

4 servings

Blend water and crumbled bread in a large bowl. Let the mixture stand for 10 minutes. While it stands, chop the pickles and the anchovies. Mash with a hand blender. You can also buy minced fish in the store. Stir this in together with capers when the bread blend is done resting.

Use a tablespoon to shape the batter into cakes and fry the fish cakes golden brown on low heat. Serve with salad and squeezed lemon.

Sophia's linguini with crab

4 servings

Another dish that has been able to stand the test of time. Our friend Sophia usually serves this. We are always impressed.

Let the crabmeat drain in a sieve. Boil the pasta and finely chop the coriander and parsley.

Blend crab meat, coriander, parsley, olive oil, salt, and pepper in a large bowl. Squeeze the lemon and add the juice to the bowl as well. Carefully warm the mixture in olive oil on medium heat in a skillet.

Pour the water out of the linguini. Blend the pasta with the crab sauce and serve.

2 cans of fine crab meat
1 pack of linguini pasta
1 plant pot of coriander
1 handful of flat-leaf parsley
¼ cup (60 ml) olive oil
salt
pepper
2 lemons

for an extra kick
fresh red chili
capers

Tuna salad

4 servings

2 cans tuna fish in water
1 red onion or 3 shallots
½ cup (60 g) pickles
1 cup (210 g) soy yogurt
2 tbsp egg-free mayonnaise
2 tbsp capers
salt
pepper
4 slices of dark bread

A classic! But the onion may not always be so popular with the kids. My tip is to make two salads. One with onions and one without.

Open the tuna cans and drain out the water.

Peel and chop the onion. Chop the pickles as well. Blend tuna, onion, pickles, soy yogurt, mayonnaise, and capers. Salt, pepper, and serve the salad on bread, preferably dark.

Quick salmon sandwiches

4 servings

This dish isn't really a specific recipe you need to follow. Rather it is meant as a source of inspiration for how quickly you can throw together a meal that is both healthy and delicious.

Toast the bread unless it is fresh out of the oven.

Mash the avocado and spread it on the bread instead of butter. Place a slice of smoked salmon on each slice of bread. Salt, pepper, and flavor with squeezed lemon.

4 slices of sourdough bread or
country bread
1 avocado
4 slices of smoked salmon
salt
pepper
1 lemon

Lightly fried fish filet with vegetables

4 servings

Remember to enjoy vegetables when they are in season. Take that extra stroll down to the market or to the vegetable stand around the corner. And fresh fish is a completely different taste experience than frozen fish that has travelled around half the globe.

Rinse the fish and dry it with some paper towels. Put it aside for now. Blend flour, breadcrumbs, and spices in a bowl. Empty the blend out on a plate that is large enough to turn the fish filets in. Dip the filets in the blend.

Rinse the spinach and boil the asparagus. Arrange spinach, asparagus, and sundried tomatoes directly on the dinner plates. If you have leftovers, you can place them in a salad bowl for seconds. Mix the ingredients for the dressing.

Fry the filets on low heat in milk-free margarine. Place the fish on the bed of fresh vegetables and top it off with the dressing. Squeeze lemon or lime on top. Serve right away.

4 fish filets
about 5 oz (150 g) per person of cod, haddock, or hake
2 tbsp flour
4 tbsp milk-free breadcrumbs
thyme
salt
pepper
2 tbsp milk-free margarine (for frying)

1 bag of fresh leaf spinach
fresh or frozen asparagus
4–6 sundried tomatoes
1 lime or lemon

dressing
1 cup (210 g) soy yogurt
2 tbsp egg-free mayonnaise
1–2 tbsp capers
salt
pepper

Shrimp pie with spinach

4 servings

It is easy to make the pie. Use this base recipe and vary the filling.

Start with the pie dough, as it needs to rest in the refrigerator for at least 1 hour. Blend flour, salt, and the milk-free margarine. Add cold water and knead to make dough. Flatten the dough, place in a pie dish, and put the dish in the refrigerator. Peel the shrimps and set the oven to 400°F (200°C).

Let the frozen spinach thaw in a saucepan on low heat for a little while. Then, squeeze out any superfluous liquid with your hands.

Pre-bake the pie bottom for 10 minutes. While it bakes, blend tofu cream cheese with soy or oat milk and spinach into a batter. Add the shrimps and spice with grated nutmeg, salt, and pepper.

Remove the pie bottom from the oven and cover with the shrimp and spinach batter. Bake the pie for another 20 minutes. Serve warm, preferably with a salad.

pie dough
1 cup (120 g) wheat flour
½ cup (60 g) spelt flour
salt
½ cup (100 g) milk-free margarine
1–2 tbsp water

filling
½ lb (200 g) shrimp
4 cups (400 g) spinach
6 tbsp (100 g) tofu soft cheese
½ cup (125 ml) soy or oat milk
½ nutmeg, grated
salt
pepper

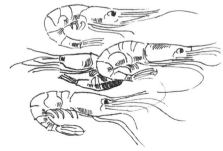

Shrimp and black rice spiced with leeks and apples

4 servings

black rice
10.5 oz (300 g) fresh shrimp, or canned
1 leek
2 red apples
olive oil
1 tsp curry
1 tsp cumin
1 cup (250 ml) water

A simple dish that feels exotic when prepared with black rice. The black rice is grown in the tropics just like other rice varieties, but it has a unique and somewhat stickier texture.

Black rice takes a while to boil, so begin early. Peel the fresh shrimps. Shrimps from a can are placed in a sieve so that the liquid drains off.

Rinse and cut the leek and apples into ½-inch (1-cm) cubes. Brown the pieces in olive oil on medium heat with curry and cumin until they are soft. Pour the water in a pan and let it come to a boil.

Add the shrimps right before serving. But make sure that they do not boil; if they do, they will turn rubbery. Salt, pepper, and serve the shrimp sauce with the rice.

Fish wrapped in foil

4 servings

This looks so professional. Yet it is so easy. Especially if you have some leftover potatoes from the day before.

Rinse the fish and pat dry with a paper towel.

Set the oven to 435°F (225°C). Rinse and shred the leeks. Make a slit in each potato and slice the carrots very thinly. If the carrots are too thick they won't have time to cook all the way through.

Place the fish on a piece of aluminum foil, large enough to wrap it. Wrap the fish around the leek shreds. Place the carrots and potatoes on either side of the fish. Season with salt and pepper. Fold the edges of the foil upward a bit and drizzle the olive oil on top.

Fold the foil packet together and bake in the oven for about 15 minutes.

4 fresh fish filets
about 5 oz (150 g) per person
½ leek
4–8 boiled potatoes
2 carrots
salt
pepper
2 tbsp olive oil flavored with lemon

Fish and chips Swedish-style

4 puff pastry sheets

8 smaller fish filets
about 2.5 oz (75 g) each pollock or cod

potatoes (firm)

salt

olive or canola oil

Mayonnaise sauce
1 cup (210 g) soy yogurt
2 tbsp egg-free mayonnaise
a few drops of lime
salt
pepper

some mild vinegar (optional)

4 servings

Here is a different version of the traditional fish and chips. Wrap the fish filets in puff pastry made without milk or eggs.

Take the puff pastry sheets out of the freezer and let them thaw on wax paper. Rinse the fish filets and dry them with a paper towel.

Set the oven to 435°F (225°C). Peel the potatoes, cut them in wedges, and salt them. Prepare by either frying the potatoes in olive oil on medium heat or baking them in the oven on a baking sheet for about 20 minutes. Drizzle olive oil on top and turn the potatoes halfway through baking time. Serve the potatoes with a little vinegar.

Roll out the puff pastry and cut each sheet into two pieces. Place a fish filet on each puff pastry sheet and fold into a packet. Press the edges together carefully. Brush with water or oil. Place the fish packets in a baking pan in the middle of the oven. Bake for about 20 minutes. While the fish bakes, blend the mayonnaise sauce for dipping. Stir the soy yogurt and mayonnaise together. Flavor with a few drops of squeezed lime, salt, and pepper. Serve right away.

Meat and fowl

Citrus-stuffed chicken

4 servings

1 orange
1 lemon
1 fresh chicken, about 2½ lb (1 kg)
canola or olive oil
dried or fresh rosemary
salt
pepper

salad or
potatoes

Rinse the orange and lemon and cut them into wedges. Keep the peels. Rinse the chicken and pat it dry with a paper towel. Grease a baking pan with some oil and set the oven to 350°F (180°C).

Spice the inside of the chicken with rosemary, salt, and pepper. Now stuff the chicken with the orange and lemon wedges, squeezing out a bit of juice. Put on a rubber glove if you find this uncomfortable. Place the chicken in the baking pan and season with salt and pepper. Bake in the middle of the oven for 80 minutes. Pour the gravy over the chicken a few times if you wish.

Serve with a large, fresh green salad or potato wedges.

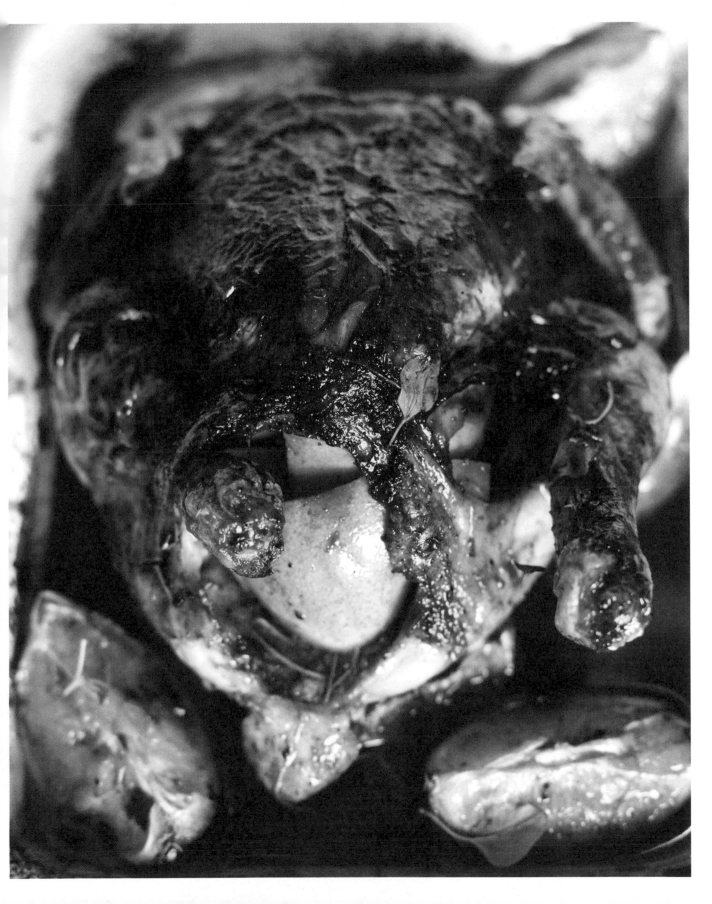

Meatballs
with mashed potatoes

4 servings

Homemade meatballs. Yes, it takes a while to make these, but there's nothing better!

Blend breadcrumbs with oat, rice, or soy milk in a bowl and let it stand for 10 minutes. Grate the onion. Peel the potatoes and place them on the stove for boiling.

Prepare the sauce. First pour the flour in a small bowl. Then add some oat or soy cream, a little bit at the time, until you have an even batter. If you add everything at once the sauce might get lumpy.

Now blend minced meat, spices, and onions in the breadcrumb blend. Shape the meat into small balls and fry on medium heat until they are cooked all the way through. Save the gravy. Let it simmer for a couple minutes.

Pour some water into the pan and whisk in with the gravy. The gravy is what creates the great taste of the sauce. Add the flour blend, soy, meat bouillon, and soy milk. Let everything simmer for a few minutes.

Mash the boiled potatoes and blend with the milk alternative and the milk-free butter. Season.

Serve with lingonberry jam and pickles.

meatballs
¼ cup (15 g) milk-free breadcrumbs
⅔ cup (170 ml) oat, rice, or soy milk
1 yellow onion (optional)
1 lb (500 g) ground pork
salt
pepper
thyme
pimento
milk-free margarine (for frying)

mashed potatoes
6–8 potatoes
1 cup (150 ml) oat or soy milk
5 tbsp milk-free margarine
black pepper
salt

sauce
2 tbsp wheat flour
½ cup (70 g) oat or soy cream
1 cup (250 ml) water and meat gravy
1 tsp soy sauce
1 meat bouillon cube
½ cup (125 ml) soy milk

Reindeer hash
with cloudberry and lingonberry
chutney

4 servings

Thaw the reindeer meat. Chanterelles from a can are placed in a sieve so that the liquid drains. Prepare the chutney. Chop the chili and red onion. Blend it with lingonberries, cloudberry jam, and spices. Flavor with lime juice.

Peel and chop the root vegetables. Fry them in the margarine with the chanterelles until they have a nice color and have softened. Move them onto a try and set aside.

Fry the reindeer meat on medium heat. Then add the root vegetables and the chanterelles to the pan to warm.

Arrange on a serving platter. Serve with chutney and grated or wedged potatoes.

1 package frozen reindeer meat, or venison
3⅓ cups (200 g) chanterelles (fresh or canned)
1 parsnip
1 celery root
1 leek
milk-free margarine (for frying)

chutney
1 tsp red chili
1 red onion
½ cup (50 g) fresh or frozen lingonberries
½ cup (15 g) cloudberry jam
½ tsp cumin
salt
pepper
1 lime

potatoes

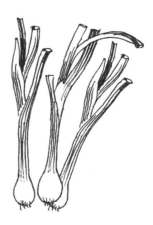

Chicken salad with fruits and greens

4 servings

The secret to really good salads is often the dressing and fresh, quality ingredients.

Rinse the salad and tomatoes or grapes. Peel and chop the mango and scallions. Set the oven to 260°F (125°C).

Dry the chicken filets with a paper towel. Fry them rapidly on high heat in a generous amount of oil or milk-free margarine so that they obtain a nice golden color. Season with salt and pepper. Move them onto a baking pan and let them bake all the way through in the oven, about 15 minutes. This makes a juicy chicken.

Roast the pine nuts and pumpkin seeds in a dry skillet on medium heat. Sprinkle with salt and set aside.

Cut the chicken filets into bite-size pieces. Blend chicken, fruit, and vegetables. Sprinkle the nuts and seeds on top.

Make a dressing out of olive oil, balsamic vinegar, and Dijon mustard. Press the garlic and add along with salt and pepper.

Pour the dressing over the salad right before serving.

1 lettuce head
(or 1 bag of mixed lettuce)
1 box of cocktail tomatoes
or seedless grapes
1 mango (fresh or frozen)
1 handful of scallions
2–3 chicken filets
2 tbsp pine nuts
2 tbsp pumpkin seeds

olive oil or milk-free margarine
sea salt
pepper

dressing
½ cup (125 ml) olive oil
2 tbsp balsamic vinegar
1 tbsp Dijon mustard
1 pressed garlic wedge
salt
pepper

Chicken nuggets with coconut

4 servings

1½ cups (120 g) jasmine rice
½ cup (35 g) grated coconut
½ cup (32 g) milk-free breadcrumbs
salt
pepper
4 chicken filets
1 pot of fresh mint
olive or canola oil
1 lemon

dip
½ cup (100 g) soy yogurt
1 tbsp sweet chili sauce
2 tsp curry
salt

Boil the jasmine rice as directed on the package. Blend grated coconut, breadcrumbs, salt, and pepper on a serving plate. Cut the chicken filets into small pieces and dip them in the coconut blend. Pick the leaves off the mint.

Mix the soy yogurt and sweet chili sauce. Flavor the dip with curry and salt.

Fry the chicken pieces on low heat in a generous amount of oil. Serve with rice, some squeezed lemon, and dip. Garnish with the mint.

Spaghetti carbonara

4 servings

1 lb (500 g) spaghetti
10.5 oz (300 g) bacon
(alternatively ham)
½ cup (125 ml) soy, rice, or oat milk
½ cup (70 g) oat or soy cream
1 tsp grated nutmeg
salt
pepper
1 cup (160 g) green peas

This is an absolute hit with children. Boil, fry, blend, and it's ready!

Boil a generous amount of water in a large saucepan. Add the spaghetti
when the water is boiling. Cut or slice the bacon into small pieces.
Fry the bacon pieces until they are crispy. Place them on a paper towel
that will absorb the excess fat. Empty the spaghetti into a sieve so that
the water drains off.

Blend soy milk, oat cream, and spices. Pour the blend over the pasta and
let it boil while stirring on medium heat. Stir in the bacon bits and, lastly,
add the peas at the end of the cooking time.

Pies with a savory filling

4 servings

Take out the puff pastry sheets ahead of time so they can thaw and set the oven to 435°F (225°C). Peel, chop, and brown the onion. Place it on a serving plate. Then fry the ground meat all the way through. Roughly chop the olives. Crumble the bouillon cube in a skillet and add the onion along with the tomato pure, olives, soy, sugar, and seasoning. Dilute with water and let the liquid evaporate while boiling. Let the blend cool.

Roll out the puff pastry and divide it into two even parts. Distribute the cooled ground meat sauce on the sheets and fold to make small packets. Press the edges together carefully. Brush with water or oat, rice, or soy milk. Place the pies on a greased baking pan and bake in the middle of the oven for 10–15 minutes. Serve with a green salad.

1 packet of puff pastry sheets
1 yellow onion
milk-free margarine
14 oz (400 g) ground meat
½ cup (35 g) green olives
1 beef bullion cube
2 tbsp tomato puree
2 tbsp soy
1 tsp sugar
1 tsp thyme
1 tsp oregano
salt
pepper
1 cup (250 ml) water
oat, rice, or soy milk

Minced lamb steaks
with jasmine rice and tzatziki

1 lb (500 g) minced lamb
1 cup (250 ml) water
¼ cup (45 g) milk-free breadcrumbs
½ cup (60 g) pickles
½ cup (45 g) preserved beets
1 yellow onion
2 tbsp fresh rosemary
2 tbsp Dijon mustard
salt
pepper
milk-free margarine (for frying)
8 skewers

jasmine rice

tzatziki
1 cucumber
salt
1 cup (210 g) soy yogurt
1 pressed garlic clove

4 servings

We blend the best right into the minced meat: red beets, pickles, and rosemary.

First make the tzatziki. Peel and grate a fresh cucumber. Place the grated cucumber in a sieve and sprinkle some salt on top. Place something heavy on top and let it sit for as long as possible. This way the liquid is squeezed out of the cucumber and the tzatziki will be nice and creamy. Afterwards, blend the cucumber with the soy yogurt and pressed garlic clove.

Thaw the minced meat at room temperature and soak the skewers. Blend the water and breadcrumbs in a large bowl and let soak for 10 minutes. While it expands, roughly chop the cucumber and beets. Finely chop the onion and rosemary. Add all of the ingredients to the breadcrumb blend and mix well. Season.

With a large spoon, scoop the meat into one hand and shape into small logs. Stick a skewer through each log and place them in the refrigerator. Let them sit for about 15 minutes. This way they will maintain their shape better while frying.

Boil the jasmine rice and fry the logs on low heat. Keep turning them so that they are cooked evenly. Serve with rice, tzatziki, and salad.

BLT
Bacon, Lettuce & Tomato

4 servings

The first printed recipe for the BLT sandwich is from the 1920s. Certain dishes never cease to amaze.

Fry the bacon until it is really crispy and place it on a paper towel to absorb the excess fat.

Peel the onion and avocado. Slice the avocados and tomatoes and cut the onion into leaf-thin rings. Rinse the salad. Make a dressing out of mayonnaise and soy yogurt. Flavor with red pepper, basil, and salt.

White bread can be toasted before you add the butter. Or even better— fry the bread in some milk-free margarine or olive oil.

Place a salad leaf on each slice of bread. Arrange the avocado, tomato, bacon, and onion on top of the leaf. Lastly add the dressing. Salt, pepper, and serve.

1 package of bacon
1 red onion
2 avocados
2 tomatoes
iceberg or romaine lettuce
4 slices of bread (dark or white)
milk-free margarine

dressing
1 tbsp egg-free mayonnaise
½ cup (100 g) soy yogurt
red pepper
fresh basil
salt
pepper

Hot sandwiches

4 servings

8 tbsp soy cream cheese
2 tbsp mustard (optional)
8 slices of bread
4 sliced tomatoes
or 8 pineapple rings
8 slices of smoked ham

Green or black olives (optional)
Grated soy cheese (optional)

A fast meal that's perfect for dinner.

Set the oven to 435°F (225°C). Spread soy cream cheese, and optionally mustard, on each bread slice. Slice the tomatoes. Layer ham with tomatoes or pineapple. Olives are also great to cut in half and add to the sandwiches. Top it off with grated soy cheese. Place the sandwiches on a baking sheet or on a baking grid and bake in the oven for about 10 minutes or until they have some color.

Chicken liver wrapped in bacon

4 servings

1 package frozen chicken liver
1 package bacon
pepper

Salty, crunchy bits that works both as an appetizer and a snack.

Thaw the chicken liver and remove any skins. Cut it into medium-sized pieces.

Wrap the liver pieces in bacon and fasten each one with a toothpick. Preheat a frying pan on medium heat. Fry carefully and continually turn the pieces so that they obtain a nice golden color and are cooked all the way through, which should take 7–8 minutes. Season with pepper.

Pizza
for every taste

4 servings

We often make pizza when we have friends over. It is especially fun when there are small children as well. We then arrange all the ingredients for toppings in different bowls and let the children make their own pizza.

Remember that the dough will need time to rise. Pizza takes a while to bake, but it's not complicated to make. You can also buy finished pizza mixes free of both eggs and milk. Or you can buy a pre-made tomato sauce.

If you wish to make your own tomato sauce you should begin with the sauce so that it will have time to cool. Finely chop the onion and brown it in milk-free margarine. Add crushed tomatoes, tomato pure, and flavor with spices. If you bought tomato sauce you can start making the dough.

Warm ¼ cup (60 ml) of water to 98°F (37°C). Dissolve the yeast in the lukewarm water. Stir in about 2 tablespoons of the flour so that you have an even batter. Let the yeast rise under a kitchen towel for about 30 minutes. While the dough is rising, chop and arrange the various toppings.

Add the remaining flour and water with the salt when the dough is finished rising. Remember to save some flour for rolling out the dough later on. Knead carefully but continuously for 10 minutes. When the dough is smooth and ready, divide it into four equal parts. Shape the parts into buns and place them under a kitchen towel so they can double in size, about 1 hour. Set the oven to 525°F (275°C).

Roll out the dough on a piece of parchment paper or a greased baking sheet. Add your toppings of choice. Finish with sliced tomatoes. The slices provide a creaminess that compensates for the lack of real cheese. Bake the pizza in the middle of the oven for 10 minutes. If the baking sheet is preheated the pizza bottom will be crispier.

Drizzle some olive oil over the baked pizza and garnish with fresh spices.

Dough
1 cup (250 ml) water
1⅓ tbsp (25 g) yeast
3½ cups (400 g) wheat flour
1 tsp salt

Tomato sauce
1 yellow onion
milk-free margarine
1 can of crushed tomatoes
2 tbsp tomato pure
salt
pepper
1 tbsp oregano
1 tbsp basil

Ideas for toppings
fresh tomatoes (instead of cheese)
tofu mozzarella
ham
pineapple
artichokes
olives
anchovies
capers
fresh basil or oregano

Fried bacon and vegetables

4 servings

1 lb (500 g) mixed root vegetables (potatoes, celery root, parsnip, carrots)

14 oz (400 g) bacon

olive oil
fresh thyme
salt
pepper
lemon

pickled cucumbers
preserved red beets

Peel the root vegetables and chop them into small pieces or buy a bag of precut vegetables. It will taste extra good if one bite contains many root vegetable flavors.

Fry the bacon until it's crispy. Place on a paper towel so that any excess fat is absorbed.

Fry the vegetables in olive oil and season with thyme, salt, and pepper. Arrange the root vegetables on a plate and squeeze the lemon juice on top. Finish off with the bacon. Serve with pickles and preserved red beets.

Poor man's saltimbocca

4 servings

I suggest preparing rice, potatoes, or salad before you start cooking the meat. This allows you to concentrate on the meat when you are frying it.

Thinly sliced steaks are fried as is, while pork filets need to be sliced into 3-inch-long (8 cm) pieces. Place a sheet of plastic wrap over the meat and pound the meat with a clenched fist. Very thick pieces should be sliced before you start pounding them.

Preheat a skillet with olive oil on relatively high heat. Add the meat when the oil is really hot. Fry the thinly sliced steaks for about 8 minutes on each side, and the pork filet a tad bit longer.

Place prosciutto and a few leaves of sage on each piece of meat, while still in the pan. Season with salt and pepper. Pour the wine on top and let it boil under a lid for 3 minutes. Serve right away with potatoes, rice, or salad.

4 medium-sized, thinly sliced steaks, or 1⅓ lb (600 g) pork filet about 5 oz (150 g) per person
4 tbsp olive oil
4 slices of prosciutto
8 sage leaves
salt
pepper
½ cup (125 ml) dry white wine

Stir-fried meat and vegetables

4 servings

A flavorful and quick dish, perfect for those days when you are craving something spicy.

Fry the chicken or beef in olive oil on high heat. Dry the skillet with paper towels and add more olive oil. Now brown the vegetables, the same way as the meat, quickly and on high heat. Add teriyaki sauce and water and let the blend simmer for a couple of minutes.

Cut the chili into thin slices and stir in with the soy yogurt. Add the lime juice. Season with salt and pepper.

Place the chicken or meat back into the skillet with the vegetables to reheat. Serve with the chili yogurt.

14 oz (400 g) chicken or beef
olive or canola oil
1 bag stir-fried vegetables
(3⅓ cups/500 g)
4 tbsp teriyaki sauce
½ cup (125 ml) water

chili yogurt
chili (without seeds)
1 cup (210 g) soy yogurt
juice of 1 lime
salt
pepper

Warm potato salad

4 servings

This salad is made with the leftovers from last night's dinner, but that doesn't mean it's not delicious. Use whatever you have at home. The salad is just as good with cold potatoes as it is with warm potatoes.

Unless you have leftovers from the day before, boil the potatoes. Cut them into small pieces. Peel and slice the onion. Chop or slice the remaining ingredients. Carefully toss everything in a large bowl. Drizzle some olive oil on top. Season with salt and pepper.

about 10 potatoes
1 red onion or leek

ham, salami, or spicy sausage
tomater
cucumber
olives
capers

fresh herbs
(for instance basil, parsley,
coriander, or lemon balm)

olive oil
salt
pepper

Kid-friendly sushi

4 servings

A perfect dish to serve the kids when you want a more adult meal yourself.

Boil the rice. Shape the ready-boiled rice into small balls.

Cut the sausage on the sides and fry it in the margarine. Place the sausage slices on the rice balls.

Cut the raw vegetables into sticks and serve with dip, ketchup, and a party mood.

1½ cups (230 g) jasmine rice
⅗ lb (300 g) sausage
ketchup
milk-free margarine (for frying)

Side snacks
carrots
cucumber
bell pepper

Dip
1 cup (210 g) soy yogurt
2 tbsp egg-free mayonnaise
lemon

Balsamic vinegar chicken

4 servings

With a delicious syrup-like sauce made from red apples, sugar, and balsamic vinegar.

Rinse the salad and finely chop the apples. Arrange the salad on each plate and set the apple pieces aside for now.

Flatten the chicken filets by covering them with a piece of plastic wrap and pounding them with your hand.

Preheat a skillet on medium heat with a generous amount of milk-free margarine. Fry the chicken on both sides so that it cooks all the way through. Save the sauce in the pan, but remove the chicken. Now add all of the apples to the pan along with sugar and vinegar. Save a few apple pieces for the garnish. Let the blend simmer until it obtains a syrup-like texture. Season with salt and pepper.

Place the chicken filets on the bed of salad and drizzle the syrup on top. Top it off with a few apple pieces.

mixed salad
2 red apples
4 chicken filets
milk-free margarine (for frying)
1 tbsp sugar
3 tbsp balsamic vinegar
salt
pepper

Chicken
with green curry

1 red bell pepper
1 bunch of broccoli
or 1⅔ cups (250 g) frozen broccoli
3 tbsp green curry
1 cup (250 ml) oat milk
1–2 tbsp fish sauce
2 lime leaves
1 can of drained bamboo shoots
1 large can of coconut milk
4 chicken filets

serving suggestions
jasmine rice
or noodles

4 servings

An incredibly simple dish that always ends up tasting great. It is not very spicy so it will work for children as well. But you may of course add more curry if you prefer. Make sure that the coconut milk does not contain cow milk, as some brands may include it.

Prepare the noodles or rice.

Cut the bell pepper and broccoli into pieces. Place all of the ingredients, except the chicken, in a saucepan and let it simmer for about 5 minutes. While it simmers, cut the chicken into small pieces and let them simmer in the blend for 8–10 minutes.

Tandoori chicken

4 servings

1 bag of tandoori spice ready mix
1 cup (210 g) soy yogurt
4 chicken filets
poppadoms (Indian chips)
oil
salt
pepper
8 grill skewers

garnish
pumpkin seeds
oil
1 tsp garam masala
2 passion fruits

raita sauce
4 tbsp tofu cream cheese
2 tbsp soy yogurt
2 tbs chopped mint
1 tsp honey

basmati rice

We live in an amazing time where all we have to do to taste the flavors from the other side of the globe is visit the grocery store and buy the spices.

Blend the tandoori spice mix with the yogurt and place the chicken filets in the spiced yogurt to marinate for 1 hour. Soak the skewers.

Stick the marinated chicken filets on the skewers. Place them in a baking pan and bake them in the middle of the oven at 350°F (180°C) for about 25 minutes. Cut the filets down the middle if they are too large. Let the rice boil while you are baking the chicken in the oven.

Roast the pumpkin seeds in a preheated dry frying pan until they get some color. Add a bit of oil and the garam masala and stir. Let the blend rest to let the flavors intensify.

Brush the poppadoms with olive oil and place them in the oven. These bake quickly so make sure that they do not burn.

Blend all of the ingredients for the sauce. Stir the cream cheese and soy yogurt together. Chop the mint and add to the sauce as well. Flavor with honey.

Serve the chicken with basmati rice, raita sauce, and poppadoms. Sprinkle pumpkin seeds on top and garnish with passion fruit halves.

Ratatouille
with couscous and spicy sausage

4 servings

water	A perfect dish when you are short on time, but still want a warm
couscous	homemade meal.
salt	
pepper	Start by boiling water. Pour the boiling water over the couscous and
4 spiced sausages	let it stew while you warm the sausage and ratatouille in a saucepan.
about 6 inches (15 cm) long	If needed, add some water and flavor with salt and pepper.
2 cans of ratatouille	
(French vegetable blend)	Drizzle olive oil over the ready couscous and stir. Serve warm.
olive oil	
	The canned ratatouille is a nice alternative to boiled vegetables.
homemade ratatouille	If you have more time you can also make a simple homemade ratatouille.
2 eggplants	
salt	Start by washing the eggplants. Cut them into pieces of about ¼ inch
2 zucchinis	(½ cm) in thickness. Place them in a sieve and sprinkle some salt on top.
3 bell peppers	The salt absorbs the fluids. Place something heavy on top and let it sit for
2 yellow onions	about 1 hour. Dry with a paper towel.
3 tbsp oil	
2 cans crushed tomatoes	Pit the zucchinis and the bell peppers and dice all of the vegetables.
2 bay leaves	Put everything in the saucepan with olive oil and sliced eggplant.
3 crushed garlic cloves	Add the crushed tomatoes, bay leaves, crushed garlic, and sugar; season
1 tbsp sugar	with salt and pepper.
salt	
pepper	Let the blend simmer on low heat under a lid until the vegetables are
	soft, for about 30 minutes.

Steak salad
with exotic flavors

4 servings

A much simpler dish than the classic Italian steak salad, but still both rich and flavorful.

Rinse the salad and thinly slice the onion. Finely chop the chili, removing the seeds. Prepare the dressing by mixing oil, vinegar, lime juice, beef broth, and liquid honey. Cut open the passion fruit and scoop out the meat. Add to the dressing. Peel and crush the garlic. Season with salt and pepper.

Quickly fry the meat on relatively high heat in margarine. Add teriyaki sauce, fish sauce, chili, and sesame oil and let it cook for a couple of minutes. Save the broth for the sauce.

Cut open the pomegranate and scoop out the seeds. Mix lettuce, sprouts, pomegranate, and the sliced onion with the meat. Serve with the dressing.

For a more filling meal, boil and add quinoa. Serve the salad warm or lukewarm.

1 bag mixed salad

1 red onion or 2 shallots

⅘ lb (400 g) thinly sliced steak

milk-free margarine (for frying)

2 tbsp teriyaki sauce

1 tbsp fish sauce

1 tsp chopped chili

a few drops of sesame oil

1 box of sprouts of your choice

1 pomegranate (optional)

quinoa (optional)

dressing

¼ cup (60 ml) olive oil

2 tsp balsamic vinegar

squeezed lime

1 tbsp liquid honey

2 passion fruits

1 garlic clove

salt

pepper

beef broth

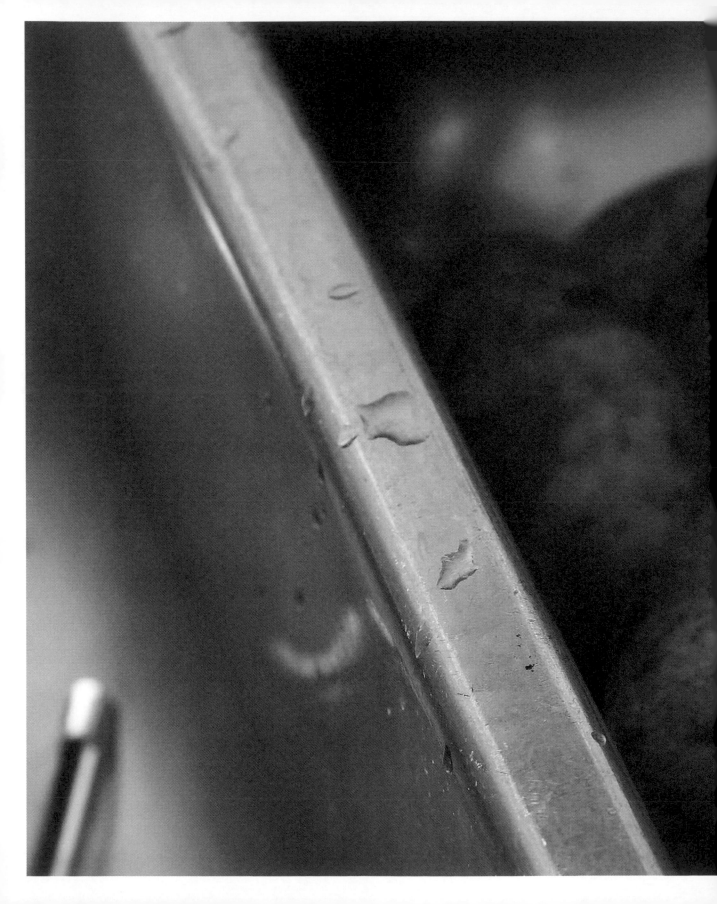

Vegetarian

Pernilla's delicious potato and leek soup

4 servings

8 potatoes
1 large leek
5 cups (1 liter) water
1 vegetable bouillon cube
2 tbsp fresh thyme
salt
pepper
3 tbsp olive oil
½ cup (70 g) oat or soy cream

Potatoes were initially cultivated by the Inca Indians in South America and were introduced in Europe during the 1700s. Imagine how different our cuisine would be without this small plant.

Peel and slice the potatoes and dice the leek. Boil water and the bouillon cube with the potatoes and leek. Lower the heat and let it simmer for about 20 minutes. When the potatoes are cooked, pour about half of the broth into a jug. You will use this later to give the soup the right texture. Pick the leaves off the thyme bush.

Mash the potato blend with a hand mixer or a fork. Add broth until the soup achieves the desired thickness.

Add the spices, olive oil, and oat cream. Serve with tasty crisp bread.

Spinach balls
rolled in sesame seeds

4 servings

Take out the spinach so that it thaws. Squeeze out as much of the liquid as possible from the thawed spinach. This is most easily done with your hands. Chop the spinach, unless you bought it chopped. Blend with crushed garlic, cumin, ajvar relish, salt, and pepper. Shape the spinach batter into meatball-sized balls. Roll the balls in sesame seeds and carefully place them in a skillet. Fry them in oil on medium heat.

Serve the spinach balls warm with squeezed lemon.

2½ cups (600 g) frozen spinach
1 crushed garlic clove
1 tsp cumin
1 tsp ajvar relish
salt
pepper
black and white sesame seeds
olive or canola oil
lemon

Beets with
sage and horseradish dressing

4 servings

Few things can compare to fresh, boiled red beets on a pleasant summer evening.

Rinse the red beets, but do not peel them. Cut off most of the tops, but leave about 2 inches (5 cm) of the stalk. The stalk gives the beets more flavor.

Boil the beets until soft in lightly salted water. Pick the leaves off of the sage and mix ingredients for the horseradish dressing. Quickly rinse the boiled beets in cold water before peeling them.

Dice the beets. Garnish with sage leaves and horseradish dressing. Sprinkle sesame seeds and pine nuts on top. Serve while the beets are still warm.

You may also fry the sage in milk-free margarine and season with salt. This will make it crispy like chips, and it tastes great with the red beets.

6⅔ cups (1 kg) fresh red beets
fresh sage
milk-free margarine
salt

garnish
sesame seeds
pine nuts

horseradish dressing
1½ cups (310 g) soy yogurt
3 tbsp horseradish (tubed or fresh)
2 tbsp egg-free mayonnaise
salt
pepper

Falafel
à la home

4 servings

1 bag of falafel mix
sunflower oil
4 pita breads
2 tomatoes
1 bag mixed salad
8 pepperoncini

hummus
1 can chickpeas (2½ cups/400 g)
squeezed lemon
2 pressed garlic cloves
3 tbsp olive oil
1 tbsp tahini (sesame paste)
salt, pepper, and paprika seasoning

homemade falafel
1½ cups (250 g) dried chickpeas
1 small red onion
2 garlic cloves
2 tsp dried coriander
2 tsp ground cumin
1 pinch cayenne
1 tsp salt
1 tsp baking powder
3 tbsp chopped, fresh parsley

sides
black olives
rice dolmas

This dish is not typically made at home as it has become a very common fast food. But it is simple, healthy, and fun to eat together.

Begin by making the hummus, unless you bought it ready-made. You can buy the hummus pre-made and naturally egg- and milk-free in most grocery stores. But making it at home always gives the best results.

Rinse the chickpeas in a sieve. Place them in a bowl that fits your hand mixer. Add the remaining ingredients and mix into a smooth batter. Add lemon if it seems too thick. If the lemon is not enough, you may also add olive oil or water. Top it off with some paprika seasoning and olive oil.

Turn on the oven and prepare the falafel buns. The simplest way is to use a falafel mix and just add water. You can use additional spices as well. Fry in sunflower oil as directed on the package. Warm the pita breads in the oven. Fill them with falafel, salad, sliced tomato, and pepperoncini. Serve with olives and rice dolmas.

Homemade falafel
Soak the chickpeas overnight. Do not use chickpeas from a can. Mash the drained chickpeas in a mixer. Add chopped onion, pressed garlic, spices, salt, baking powder, and parsley and continue mixing. Pour a generous amount of sunflower oil into a thick-bottomed saucepan and heat it. Shape the chickpea mass into small buns with a spoon. Carefully place the buns in the oil and fry for 3–4 minutes until they are golden brown. Keep a lid close by in case the saucepan catches fire. Let excess fat run off on a paper towel and serve the falafel warm.

Hash browns
with olives and chanterelles

4 servings

Let the chanterelles drain in a sieve. Fresh chanterelles need to be rinsed carefully. Brown them in milk-free margarine. Season with salt and pepper and set aside. Slice the onion thinly. Peel and grate the potatoes on the rough side of the grating iron.

Spice the grated potato with cumin, salt, and pepper. Shape the blend into small buns, the size of a potato. Place them two at the time in a preheated skillet with a large spoonful of milk-free margarine. Press down with a spatula to flatten them.

Fry on medium heat on each side. If you find it hard to turn them, place them first on a small plate and press the plate against another plate, then place the hash brown back into the pan. They are ready when they are golden brown and crispy along the edges. Feel free to place the hash browns in the oven at 210°F (100°C) to keep them warm until serving.

Top with chanterelles, olives, red onion, and soy crème fraiche.

2⅕ lbs (1 kg) firm potatoes
2 tsp whole cumin
salt
pepper
milk-free margarine (for frying)

topping
5 cups (300 g) chanterelles
(fresh or canned)
milk-free margarine
1 red onion
20 green olives
4–5 tbsp soy crème fraiche
salt and pepper

lingonberry jam (optional)

Jerusalem artichoke soup

4 servings

4 cups (600 g) Jerusalem artichoke
3 cups (750 ml) water
1 tbsp squeezed lemon
1 finely-chopped red onion
milk-free margarine (for frying)
2 cups (500 ml) water
½ cup (125 ml) dry white wine
1 bouillon cube
1 cup (210 g) oat or soy cream
salt
pepper

The Jerusalem artichoke is a great little root vegetable that belongs to the composite plant species. The flower looks like a sunflower. With wine and spices this root transforms into a delicious soup.

Peel and dice the Jerusalem artichoke. Place the pieces directly in the water with the squeezed lemon juice. This way they will not darken but maintain their light color.

Brown the onion carefully in a larger saucepan in milk-free margarine. Add the artichoke pieces, the 2 cups of water, wine, and bouillon cube. Bring it to a boil under a lid and let it simmer until the artichoke pieces are soft. About 15 minutes.

Mix the blend into a smooth soup with the help of, for instance, a hand mixer. Add the oat cream and boil for another 5 minutes. Add more water if you want a thinner soup. Flavor with salt and pepper. Sprinkle some chopped nuts or roasted sesame seeds on top. Serve the soup warm with tasty bread.

Spinach soup with lentils

4 servings

At one point I lived with a group of friends in London where I was a student for years. We would often eat Indian food at the most fantastic restaurants. This rich soup is inspired by that time. We had a small budget, but we ate well and had fun.

Place the frozen spinach in a saucepan and let it thaw on low heat.

Add all of the ingredients, except the coriander, and let it simmer for 10 minutes. While it simmers, warm the naan bread or another white bread.

Pick the leaves off of the coriander and add to the soup right before serving.

2⅔ cups (500 g) frozen, chopped spinach
2 cups (400 g) red or green lentils
1 vegetable bouillon cube
⅓ cup (90 g) oyster sauce
2 tbsp teriyaki sauce
1 pressed lemon
2½ cups (625 ml) water
2 naan breads
1 pot fresh coriander

Potato salad with cumin

4 servings

Our everyday potato is easily transformed into a fine delicacy.
Use crispy vegetables, tasty dressings, and a little creativity.

Start by peeling the potatoes and place them in water for boiling. Rinse
the beans and cut the stems off of the snow peas. Thinly slice the red
onion.

Roast the pine nuts and cumin in a dry skillet on medium heat. Once
the pine nuts start to brown they will burn easily, so keep a close eye on
everything and stir continuously.

Dice the cooled potatoes. Blend all of the ingredients for the salad. Stir
together the ingredients for the dressing and pour it over the salad right
before serving.

6–8 firm potatoes
2 cups (400 g) black beans
½ cup (100 g) fresh snow peas
(or 1 pack frozen snow peas)
1 red onion
8 sundried tomatoes
¼ cup (25 g) pine nuts
1 tsp whole cumin
salt
pepper

dressing
¼ cup (60 ml) olive oil
3 tbsp balsamic vinegar
1 tbsp Dijon mustard
2 pressed garlic cloves
1 tbsp liquid honey
salt
pepper

Root vegetable casserole with nutmeg and thyme

4 servings

Set the oven to 390°F (200°C). Peel and dice all of the root vegetables and the onion.

Blend soy or oat milk and soy crème fraiche with the spices. Butter a large baking pan or a couple of smaller-sized baking pans. Layer the vegetables and pour the batter on top. Finish with the thyme.

Cook the casserole in the oven for about 50 minutes. You can cover with aluminum foil after a while to make sure that it doesn't burn. If it is starting to look dry, just add more soy or oat milk.

2⅕ lb (1 kg) potatoes
3 carrots
1 small turnip
1 parsnip
2 yellow onions
thyme

1½ cups (375 ml) soy or oat milk
½ cup (100 g) soy crème fraiche
½ tsp grated nutmeg
salt
pepper

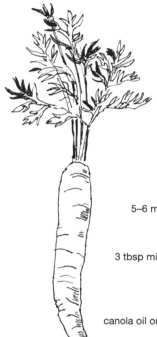

Carrot burger
with horseradish dressing

8 small burgers or 4 large

5–6 medium-sized carrots
1 yellow onion
2 tbsp water
3 tbsp milk-free breadcrumbs
1 tbsp potato flour
salt
pepper
canola oil or milk-free margarine
(for frying)

romaine lettuce
2 tomatoes
1 red onion
ciabatta bread or similar

dressing
½ cup (100 g) soy yogurt
2 tbsp soy crème fraiche
(can be left out)
2 tbsp grated horseradish
(you can find this tubed)
a few drops of lime
salt
pepper

This is our answer to the traditional burger. Vitamin-packed steaks with loads of flavor. What used to be unhealthy but delicious, is now both healthy and tasty.

Grate the carrots and the onions and place them in a large bowl. Add water, breadcrumbs, and potato flour. Mix and let it stew for 5 minutes. Mix the ingredients for the dressing, rinse the lettuce leaves, and slice the tomatoes.

Season the breadcrumb blend with salt and pepper. Shape the steaks into small hamburgers and fry them in oil or milk-free margarine on medium heat.

Place the vegetables and the cooked carrot burgers between two slices of toasted bread, preferably ciabatta. Flavor with the horseradish dressing.

Gazpacho

4 servings

A wonderfully cold soup perfect for a hot summer day. If you want, you can cut up more vegetables and make a dip so the children can enjoy some variety.

Start by peeling the cucumber and slice it. Slice the rest of the vegetables and the bread. This way it is easier to mix everything evenly.

Blend all of the ingredients and add some water. Mix with a hand mixer. Continue mixing until the soup is even and smooth without chunks. Add water until it has your desired thickness. It should be runny enough that you can drink it out of a glass. Season with salt, pepper, and some Tabasco.

Feel free to let the soup sit overnight. It will only get better.

Cut the crusts off the bread slices, dice the bread, and fry it in oil or milk-free margarine. Garnish and serve the soup cold with fried croutons.

1 cucumber
6 cups (1 kg) fresh tomatoes
(or 2 boxes of plum tomatoes)
2 green bell peppers
2 slices white bread
red onion
2 pressed garlic cloves
½ cup (125 ml) olive oil
2 tbsp red wine vinegar
1 cup (250 ml) cold water
salt
pepper
Tabasco

Garnish
2 slices of toasted white bread
olive oil or milk-free margarine

Fruit salad

4 servings

about 5⅓ cups (800 g) fruit; 1⅓ cup (200 g) per person
for instance, bananas, apples, pears, oranges, kiwi, passion fruit,
frozen or fresh raspberries
frozen or fresh blueberries
frozen or fresh mango

for a richer variety
smoked ham

topping suggestions
soy cream
tofu ice cream or oat milk ice cream
nuts
honey

Select the fruits that you like best. The amazing thing about fruit is that basically all fruit in the world tastes great together. It is most delicious if you combine at least four different kinds of fruit.

Peel and cut the fruits into medium-sized pieces. You can save the juice from the juicier fruits, like oranges, and pour it over the salad. If you have chosen less sweet fruits, such as frozen blueberries, you may flavor the salad with some honey or orange juice to really enhance the flavors.

Smoothie

1–2 servings

1½ cups (375 ml) soy milk or soy yogurt
1½ cups (180 g) berries or fruit (banana, frozen mango/ blueberries, raspberries, strawberries)

1 scoop of tofu or oat milk ice cream (optional)
mint, cinnamon, or honey nuts

The world's best breakfast or snack. You can use whatever you want to make a smoothie. If your family needs some extra vitamins, just add in some carrots. Furthermore, you can turn this into a milkshake with just a bit of imagination.

To make a smoothie you need a mixer, hand beater, or hand mixer. The easiest to use is a hand mixer.

Blend all of the ingredients and mix well until you see a smooth texture. It can be unpleasant, especially for kids, if there are still some chunks.

During summertime, when you usually eat fresh fruit, it can be nice to add a couple of ice cubes or milk-free ice cream to the smoothie for a more refreshing drink. Feel free to flavor the smoothie with spices like mint, cinnamon, or honey. Top it off with nuts.

Pancakes

4 servings

2 tbsp milk-free margarine
1 cup (120 g) wheat flour
3 tsp baking powder
1 tsp salt
1 tbsp sugar
1½ cups (375 ml) soy milk
milk-free margarine (for cooking)

topping
maple syrup
fresh or frozen thawed berries
tofu ice cream or oat milk ice cream

We love pancakes! All kinds of pancakes. In all honesty we believe that pancakes make a great dinner meal. You can definitely replace soup accompanying your dinner with these.

Melt the margarine and let it cool. Blend all of the dry ingredients in a large bowl. Pour half of the liquid ingredients into the dry ingredients and whisk quickly to make a uniform batter. Add the remaining liquids and stir well. If you add all of the liquids at once, you can easily create lumps in the batter. Lastly, add the melted margarine.

Scoop the batter into a preheated frying pan with margarine. The pancakes will rise a little, so don't place the dollops of batter too close to each other in the pan. Cook the pancakes until golden brown on medium heat. Serve right away with maple syrup, berries, and optionally milk-free ice cream or whipping cream.

Good to know

You can be sensitive to different foods for a variety of reasons—allergies, food intolerance, or just an adverse food reaction. Here you can read about what you can eat and what you cannot.

Allergies

It is the protein in the milk and the eggs that some become allergic to. This is because the natural defense mechanisms of the body do not function as they should. The body's immune system reacts to these proteins making us feel sick.

Milk protein allergy is most common in younger children who often grow out of it. Egg allergies often take hold at an older age, but also usually disappear by the early school years. Symptoms may include stomachaches, vomiting, hives, eczema, or asthma, among others.

If you suffer from multiple allergies, or when your children are still very young, you may want to visit a nutritionist to learn what foods you can eat for a well-balanced diet.

Lactose intolerance

Intolerance of lactose in cow's milk is a result of a lack of enzymes (lactase) to break up the milk sugar in the intestine. This may lead to a bloated stomach, gas, stomachaches, and diarrhea.

To make the symptoms disappear it can be enough to lower your intake of milk, but if they continue, you should use low-lactose or lactose-free foods, or stay away from lactose all together.

Adverse food reactions

Adverse food reactions may happen and they are usually reminiscent of an allergic reaction, but the cause is usually unknown.

Sometimes you can have a food reaction to foods or drinks without the involvement of the immune system. In these cases, it is another kind of food reaction. An example of this would be eczema, which many children get when they eat citrus, tomato, red or yellow candy, and certain chocolates.

Examples of products and foods that contain or may contain lactose or milk proteins.

Shortening	Milk albumin	*Semi-processed products*
Chocolate	Milk chocolate	
Crème fraiche	Milk protein	Fish sticks
Sour milk	Milk powder	Broth/ bouillon cubes
Ice cream	Milk egg whites	Hamburger
Heavy cream	Sodium caseinate	Hamburger buns
Sour cream	Nougat	Meatballs
Casein	Cheese	Liver pâté
Caseinate	Cheese powder	Burger patties
Kefir	Breadcrumbs	Pastries
Cottage cheese	Skimmed milk powder	Pizza
Coconut milk	Processed cheese	Potato croquettes
Buttermilk powder	Butter	Potato cakes
Lactose	Breadcrumb flour	Hotchpotch
Margarine	Dry milk powder	Salami
Margarine cheese	Whey	Soups
Meringues	Whey powder	Sorbet
Cooking fat	Vegetable products	Sauces
Whey cheese	Margarine	White bread
Whey butter	Baby formula	
Cream cheese	Yogurt	
Milk		

Examples of products and foods to avoid that may contain eggs

Béarnaise sauce	Bread brushed with eggs
Meat products	
Tin loaf	Potato buns
Fromage cheese	Rusks
Minced meat dishes	Sorbet
Ice cream	Breadcrumbs
Candy	Tarts
Casseroles	Waffles
Whole egg powder	Ovalbumin
Hollandaise sauce	Egg white sweets
Hen's egg whites	Egg noodles
Cakes and pastry	Egg globulin
Coconut buns	Egg yolk
Meatballs	Egg yolk powder
Liver pâté	Egg whites
Mayonnaise	Egg white powder
Mayonnaise dressings	
Meringues	
Pies	
Pasta	
Fried dishes	
Pancakes	

Products that may sound like they contain lactose or milk protein, but don't.

E numbers (in Europe)	Lactobacillus
Cocoa butter	Rennet
Calcium diglutamate	Lactic acid
Calcium lactate	Lactic acid bacteria
Potassium	Sodium lactate
Coconut milk *	Butter flavoring
Lactase	

* Carefully check the content label. Some processed coconut milks contain cow milk.

Recipe Index